Father and Son

Father and Son

MAJID NAFICY

RED HEN PRESS   LOS ANGELES

Cover photos:
"Santa Monica, Dusk" © 2003 Bob Witkowski
"Pol-e Khadjoo at Night" © 2003 IranPIX

Author Portrait by Azad Naficy at age 4

Book & Cover Design: Mark E. Cull

ISBN 1-888996-68-4

Manufactured in Canada

Publication of this volume is made possible in part
through support by the California Arts Council.

Red Hen Press
www.redhen.org

First Edition

TABLE OF CONTENTS

Father and Son

A NOTE TO THE READER

This collection contains poems created by a father who lives in exile. The first poem is written when the son was an embryo and the last just before he becomes a teenager.

Originally in Persian, they are translated into English by the poet with the help of his friend, Harriet Tannenbaum.

TO AN EMBRYO

One day
You became free,
Shaking your tail
Moving your lips:
"Water! Water!"
Miscounting her days
She heard your voice:
"Here I am!
Here I am!"
I became father
She became mother
And we both said:
"Ah, Azad fish![1]
Give us more time
Life is hard in exile.
Come back in a happy season."

On our way to a surgeon
A fire flamed in her body
And spread into my soul
Like that self-moving life cell
From which life began on the earth.
She said:
"Was there a design for it?"
And I said:
"Or any designer?"

Then comes fishing:
Choosing a name.
She says: "Azadeh"
And I say: "Or Azad"
We both laugh.

October 17, 1987

---

[1] Salmon.
Azad in Persian means "free," and is used as a name for boys. The female version
of this name is Azadeh.

FATHER AND SON

You took me by surprise, Azad!
Putting your tiny being
In the cradle of my body:
"Now, I am the son and you are the father
How long do you hope to remain
The rebellious child of this house?"
I bent over the illegible letters of your body.
With wet hair and slippery skin
You resembled a little fish
Coming from the far away ocean
And dragging this tired old whale
To the fearful undertow.
I wanted to cut the umbilical cord
But the scissors failed.
You cried out behind closed eyes:
"Dad, I am here
Don't you feel my sticky skin?"
Esmat smiled under the yellow light
Looking at the strange riddle
She had put in front of me:
Am I now closer to death
Or further from it?

At home, I set aside my philosophical riddle.
The aroma of your body is enough for me.
Your beautiful eyes talk to me
And your black bangs
Shine like a badge of courage.
Your smile is not fake
And tears simply signal your pain.
Your yawning is the booty
That your sleep steals from wakefulness.
In your refreshing burps
I find the fresh air of early morning
And in your pleasant farts
I feel the cool summer afternoons.

Oh, you poisonous gases, go out!
And let my child be calm.
"Lullaby, lullaby, my almond blossom!
Close your eyes, sleep calmly."

May 1988

THE OLD CRADLE

The old cradle testifies
That the face of my father
Who was bending toward me
Is now hovering over your head.

Where were you all these years?
I was sure it was you.
I know your clear eyes
Your beautiful dimple,
The little apple of your chin
And your faithful fists
Which disclose their secrets
Only when you yawn.

You hide behind empty bottles,
Dirty diapers and bibs
And the clothes which every hour
Become too small.

I hold you tight
You lie down on my chest
With your feet touching my belly button
And your arms hanging over my sides.
I want to live with every moment of your life
Jump with every noise of your body
And with each cramp of your tummy
Grunt, until you are emptied.

Peek-a-boo!
Peek-a-boo!
Enough of this childish game!
The old cradle testifies
That you have traveled this long path
Together with me once before.

May 1988

DEATH AND LIFE

I know that you will bury me with your hands
My corpse already weighs on your tiny shoulders
Your restless fingers supporting your milk bottles
Tomorrow will grasp my burial shovel
Your tears this time brought on by heat rash
Echo as your cryings at my death
And your jet of water wetting me head to toe
Is like the water that you will pour on my grave.
I mistake the smell of this fresh milk
For the scent of newly dug earth,
The sheet for the shroud
And the cradle for the casket.

The music of your gurgling milk
Is the most beautiful song of life.
Each drop that you swallow
Is accompanied with a breath
And half-way through each bottle
You take time out,
For your gums and restless tongue.
I wish I were a tiny finger
In your mouth of simple desires.
I wish I were a smile on your lips,
When you bloom with satisfaction.
Your feet are the end of my ambition
And your hands the firm bridge of trusts.
Every night, when I wake up
And warm your bottle of milk,
I find my wakefulness in you.
These bottles
Are not emptied and refilled in vain
The sound of your breath testifies.
Oh, death, listen!
I will thus take my revenge on you.

June 1988

17

FOGGY GROVE

In the foggy grove
My inscriptions are still visible
On the bark of black poplars.
Azad, dear!
Make a swing of your wishes
Hold your hands
And let yourself swing
Neenee, nuna
Neenee, nuna
Neenee, nuna
Be calm
Be patient
My little one!
Knowledge of life is in your hands
Let this swing get its momentum
It's not a long path
From the foggy grove
To the tough, naked desert.

One morning I started off
With Father's staff in my hand
Its polished wood caressed my skin
And like a sparkler
It sent sparks of my joy.
When I reached the hilltop
The sun's rays burned my head.
In search of a vision
I looked toward the horizon
But there was nothing visible
Except colored patches of earth.
I wanted to return, but suddenly
The scent of a flower brought me back:
"I am here,
Blooming on your chest
A tiny flower from your childhood.
Sniff my scent
And hold on to me."

Azad, dear!
Hold your hands
It's your turn.

June 1988

CHILD AND THE SEA

The sea said: "Surrender the child
The cradle of my waves is more deserving than your weary arms."
Azad in his blanket and ruffled cap
Looked like a flower
Blooming on my chest.
I bent to pick up a shell
To chase this old babbler.
Surprise! I found an empty beer bottle
On the sandy crust of the ground:
"Oh, sea, sea, sea
Is this your gift to me?
Is this that Moses
Whom you picked up from Pharaoh's court
To place at my feet
On this side of the ocean?
You passed from the open arms of my homeland,
Crowded cities of India,
Virgin jungles of Ceylon
And vast green waters
Just to mock me!
I spit on your white beard!"

Azad was calm
As if he was listening
To my conversation with the sea.
I threw away the empty bottle.
It bounced and disappeared in a wave:
"I have come from far away
From the warm waters of the Indian ocean
To my exile on this Pacific side
And now you, who connect shore to shore
Pour salt on my wounds.
Oh, you old babbler!
What do you have in your hands
That dares you to boast?
Only jagged shells and empty bottles.

In the cradle of your waves
There's no place for children of prison and exile.
There is no sign of the lost tomb of my brother
Or the shattered heart of my martyred wife.
No trace of my eyes that became impaired
No remembrance of the Revolution that was crushed.
Where is my Spring of Freedom?[2]
Where is the rebellion of shack–builders
And the uprising of petroleum workers?
Where is the shutting down of palaces
And opening of welcoming arms?
Where is the destruction of old illusion
And the creation of new vision?
What news of Evin[3] prisoners?
Or of war refugees,
Barren dreams and ruined cities,
Bleeding Kurds and shrouded women?
Curse me who waited so long
Coming every evening to welcome you
And find a remedy for my wounds
But what have I found?
Only the movement of your heedless waves."

Azad moved,
I opened his blanket
His eyes seemed brighter than ever before:
"Oh, my Azad!
My freedom!
You came into the world
In a foreign country
But, I see in your eyes
A flickering light of my homeland.
Will you sooth my wounds?
And speak of my dreams?"

---

[2] A euphoric expression often used by Iranian people after the February, 1979
Revolution.
[3] A political prison in Tehran.

Azad waved his hands
Like a capable conductor
As if he wanted to create harmony
Between the raving waves and my frantic talk:
"No, it's not fair!
Of all those bygone dreams
It has brought back an empty beer bottle.
Now I'm to surrender the child of my hope
To the cradle of its waves.
If I throw you into the water
Will it carry you to Bushehr or Mashur?
In your sealed box
Will it feed you milk
And burp you on time ?
Will it give you, as a Moses
To the people on the other shore?
Ah,my Azad!
Will it take you
To the sun-drenched alleys,
To the burned-out gardens,
To the empty plains
And the silent moutains
So that you listen to the echo
Of the child-like banter
Which once filled our friendly circle
And now is silenced in the execution fields?
Will you see the new shoots
And will you say to the tiny infants
That this exile is not sleeping
And his heart still beats with theirs?
Tell me whether this is so
I will then throw you into the water.
Perhaps I am a Pharaoh myself
And you a Moses,
Who will abandon me
To create a new vision."

With my weak hands,
I dug a pit to shelter Azad.

And I slipped into the water
In the fury of the waves
I heard the outcries of my pals
Who were executed in the Evin hills:
"No!
Why should I throw my chest-flower
Toward you, oh sea?
Why should I not be Moses?
Wrap me in the cradle of your waves
And do not scare me
With your whales and sharks.
Carry me beyond China, India and Ceylon
To the waters of the Gulf
To the ever welcoming arms of my homeland
To the naked sun
To the 'hi there's and 'howdy's
To the cool water jugs of friendship.
Oh, you old babbler
If there is a shred of strength in you
Swallow me and take me back to the other side."

When I reached the green water
I turned back and looked at Azad
In his blanket and ruffled cap.
He seemed to be asleep.
In the raging wave I saw nothing else.

July 1988

MILK TIME

Whenever it's milk time,
Azad and I chase each other.

He turns into a lamb,
Shakes his head,
Purses his lips,
Opens his mouth,
And grabs whatever is or is not.
I turn into a sheep,
All eyes, head to toe.
He becomes a tree
And with a throat full of murmuring water
Grows tall.
Grows tall.
Grows tall.
I fly like a woodpecker
Then sit on his back:
Tap tap
Tap tap
Tap tap.

When he burps
He shrinks again
And I grow big.
And the game begins again.

June 3, 1988

SECRET OF THE RIVER

Every day we go along the river
And your body
Takes on the smell of the water.

Seeing us, the wild geese
Tune up their battle horns,
And a cat behind its green hideout
Lifts his tail in triumph.
The old fishermen,
With their buckets full of sorrow
Move from place to place
And a palm frond in our way
Forces me to bend my head.

I stand still
And as you sleep on my shoulder
I think to myself:
"It's too late for me
But maybe you will find
The secret of the river."

January 10, 1989

A NOVICE MOUNTAIN CLIMBER

Cold and tough,
You were climbing down my chest,
Your legs were pounding against my hips,
As if, with your clawing hands,
You wanted to take this hollow cliff,
Into the valley of nowhere.

I was standing, asking myself,
Is he talking of this break-up?

Next time,
When we smile at each other,
Climb up from my hip
And let your head rest on my chest.
I want you, O novice mountain climber,
To make of me a proud cliff.

May 30, 1990

REPENTANCE

Oh, Lord, forgive Thou me,
Not as Thou forgavest Thy children, Eve and Adam.
They tremble still
Behind the trees of Eden,
In awe of Thy mighty strides.
And they clutch the stolen green fruit
In their small hands.

Oh, Lord, forgive Thou me,
Not as Thou forgavest Thy son, Cain
Thou didst not want his corn,
But Thou accepted Abel's herd.
So Thou provoked Cain's jealousy
And put a dagger in his fist.

Oh, Lord, forgive Thou me,
Not as Thou forgavest Thy children, the people of Noah.
Thou punished them with such a mighty flood
That to this day
The crew which was sent
To bring news from land
Has not yet returned.

Oh, Lord, forgive Thou me,
Not as I forgave my son, Azad.
He woke up at midnight, demanding milk,
But I denied him
To break this nightly habit.
He began sobbing,
And I put my hand on his mouth
To silence him.
Deep in his eyes
I felt the sound of Adam's children,
Who for centuries have moaned
Under the wrath of their own god.

Oh, Lord . . .
Nay, thou my son, forgive thou me
You forgive me.

January 4, 1991

ASTHMA

Tonight
A thousand prisoners
Are crying out in your lungs,
And there is no escape.

January 10, 1991

THE LITTLE MESSENGER

You will tell your mother
That yesterday afternoon
You went biking with me
Then you took a shower
Read alphabets
Had dinner
Slept well
And, in the morning,
Leaving my house with your backpack
You went to preschool on number one.
In the evening, your mother will pick you up
And will drive you to her house.
She will open your lunch box
And from the leftovers
Will figure out
What I've cooked for you.
You will play with your cars
Send your grandma on errands
Draw pictures with your aunt.
Then, you will flap your wings
And fly toward me.

What do you get from me?
What do you give to her?
What do you get from her?
What do you give to me?
Little messenger!
I do not want you
To fill this void.
When you are in love
There is no need
To share a roof.

May 3, 1991

I TAKE AZAD TO SCHOOL

Every morning
I take Azad to school.
Hanging around the bus stop
Veterans still continue the war.
An addict stares at Azad
From the corner of his eye,
And suddenly throws his hat
Into the street.
The bus stops short.
Azad says: "transfer!"
And waves the white slip in the air.
In the rear seat,
A woman sells her infant's milk.
Waving to the car behind
Azad changes the bus number
And shouts, in triumph, "11!"

Today is Monday, and so
He buys fortunes from the Korean shop:
"A plastic watch again!"
I ask him:
"Why do you like fortunes so much?"
And hand him his lunchbox.
He throws me a kiss behind bars.
My preschool had barred doors
And our local prison, too.

I always return by the back street.
Homes are still yawning
And smelling of tortillas and coffee.
The yellow leaves are everywhere.
I pass by the cemetery.
Pushing through bars
The vines ask me about Ezzat[4]
After the abortion, she came home

---

[4] She was my first wife.

Crying, she said:
"I killed a person!"
When she was executed,
I understood what she meant.

From the nearby freeway,
I hear cars passing
They are not visible.
I reach the little Methodist Church
All box woods are trimmed evenly.
On the window ledges, there are no flowers
And no doves sing in the entryway.
I climb the stairs
The Mexican neighbor is drunk
He plays guitar and
The Eritrean chants his lament.
For another day,
I have taken Azad to school.

September 11, 1992

SHOULDER-STRAP PURSE

From Iran my mother
Has sent Azad a purse,
Embroidered with flowers
And filled with the aroma
Of basil and bread.

In its tiny pocket,
I find sunflower seeds:
From a field facing the sun
With golden buzzing bees
And a child walking barefoot
In the nearby creek,
Blowing into a wheat stem.

Can Azad hear
The sound of that reed?

I open the seeds,
All are rotted
And taste bitter.

October 8, 1992

CHILDHOOD LANDSCAPE

I cannot see from here
My childhood landscape

Every morning, in the window frame
It was Mt. Soffeh
With its high hump
and its invisible leash
In my impatient hands.

December 29, 1992

MOUSE

If you knew that you were a mouse
With worried eyelids,
You would creep out of your cage
Behind the refrigerator
To hide in a safe hole
Beneath the cupboard.
And when the tap-tap of the broom
And 'hey! stop it!' and 'hey! catch it!'
Die down and the house becomes empty
You would peep out from behind
The old spider webs
Pass the wooden legs,
And the plastic thongs
And return to your cage
To eat from the grain dish
And drink from the water bowl
And close your eyelids.

August 4, 1993

RETURN

You put your right hand on my pillow
I lay my left cheek on your palm
You close your eyes
And I hold you with my right arm.

Your eyelids are borderless
And your hair exudes pride.
I take a wisp of your hair into my mouth
And see you in the dim light of the room
Galloping horse along with me
Passing the border into Turkey.
Your hair glows in the sun
The snow reaches halfway up your legs.
We have lost our way
The Kurdish guides are worried.
You dismount the horse
Hold the reins
And lead us to the last border village.
The Kurdish partisans wave
From their high embankment
And call back their wild dogs.
Your hair glows in the sun
And the snow melts on your shoulders.
I put my boots next to yours
And surrender my dead feet to the fireplace.
The partisans lay their oozies down on the carpet
And the room is filled with smiles and gold teeth.
I put down the hot teacup
And light my first Mal Tappeh.[5]

From the next room,
Comes the sound of the piano.
I see Azad's tiny fingers
Tripping on the black and white keys:
"Mr. Turtle see him go

---

[5] A popular cigarette in Turkey.

Walking there, kind of slow
Waddling from side to side
Going back to the sea."
I say to myself:
"You naughty boy!
Play 'Cuckoo'
Play 'Cuckoo' who is calling his old mate
In the faraway forests."

His proud hair glows in the sun
The tiny turtles drips from his fingers:
"Mr. Turtle is going back to the sea.
Mr. Turtle mi re do re
Mi la so
Fa mi re
Mi re do
Mi re do mi la so
Fa mi re mi re."

December 25, 1993

RED EARMUFFS

I saw my red earmuffs again.
We were sitting on the bus
Going home from school.
It was windy outside
The palm trees trembled.
He opened his folder
And showed his homework:
"Three scarfs
Two hats
Four gloves
And one ear . . . whatever it is."
An old man turned his head
And said: "earmuffs"
He had to color them
And count each group.
The bus was filled with words
And the windows grew frosty.

My father brought them from America
They were soft and cozy
Red on the outside and white inside
With a green headpiece in between.
We were sitting in the 'turret room.'
Father wore a sheepskin cap.
His eyes were opened wide
His hands covered his ears
Looking like a wolf in the snow.
Friday mornings, we went to Mt. Sofa.
The snow was everywhere
And I wore my red earmuffs.
We passed big bolders
And sat by the Khajik Fountain
To have our breakfast.
Father had Istanbul potatoes
Dr. Khalili, offered sour cherry jam.
Then, we leaned back toward the bolder

Watching the city's skyline.
Father smoked his once-a-week cigarette
And Mr. Varzandeh wiped his mouth
With his wide, worn-out tie.

That night as he slept
I opened his folder.
He had colored the earmuffs red,
All red.

January 6, 1994

ROCK

I broke your rock today
You broke into tears.

Everyday you held it in your fist
And boldly went to school.
No one could beat you.
On the bus, you stood on the seat
And rubbed it over the window
Like a diamond cutter,
Asking: "Can a police bullet
Break it into pieces?"

Sometimes it disappeared.
You searched your pockets
Looked high and low in the house
And, finally, found it in your bed
it appeared even in your dreams.

Today you asked me:
"Can your hammer break my rock?"
So like two rock scientists
We went to the backyard.
First, you hammered it
But it didn't break
Then, you ordered me to try.
I wish I had broken my hand
Instead of breaking your heart.
The world is full of solid rocks
But I know your tiny hands
Will not grasp a rock any more.

April 11, 1994

APPLE

Last night,
I saw you in my dream
Handing me an apple
That had a red charm
Like your dimple.

I had to take it
Toss it in the air
And place it on the mantle,
As a potpourri.
Yet, I remembered
Those nights of horror
You couldn't sleep
Gasping for air.
You closed your eyes
Behind your nebulizer,
Vanishing in the mist:
". . . And Snow White
Took the apple,
Had a bite
And went to sleep
And the seven gentle dwarfs
Put her in a glass casket . . ."
Until one day, that Greek doctor
Waved the lab report in the air
And said: "he is allergic to apples."
I bent
And kissed your lips.
You opened your eyes
And the world came alive again.

Did I take the apple?

October 12, 1994

WE ARE SITTING NEXT TO EACH OTHER

We are sitting next to each other
Scissors and comb play with our hair.
The revolving chair raises you to my level,
And the big wall mirror joins us together.
When I look at you, I see myself
When I look at me, it is you.

I wore eyeglasses back then.
Soluki's aid would take them off
I worried all the time:
Where has he put them?
The counter under the mirror
Was filled with ghostly forms:
Mug, brush and soap
Razors and clippers
And I could not find my glasses.
When I put five *rials* in his palm
He would smile and say: "Can't you see?"
And place the flexible arms around my ears.

The woman asks: "How do you want his hair cut?"
I say: "I like it short, but you'd better ask him."
You turn the pages
And show her a hair style.
I could have either a crew cut or a flat top.
But that summer, I wore sideburns
And by fall, I became a hippie.
Ajami did not like long hair.
He stood at the school gate and sent me home.
I did not go to school for a few weeks.

I say: "No hair on my ears."
And I uncover my hands from the white cape.
Son-of-a-gun always wounded my neck.
I cried silently
He wet cotton with alcohol

And put it on the cut.
He was too cheap to use a new blade.

I asked my mother:
"What if Soluki himself gave me a haircut?"
Once a month, early in the morning,
He came to our house
And put his bicycle in the hallway.
While he was giving my father a haircut,
I would bike to the end of the street
Ten times, belly-style.[6]

She gives me the hand mirror
Without looking at myself, I ask:
"Could you trim my eyebrows?"
I remove bits of hair from my face
And just as I feel the cool air
Around my ears
The woman calls me:
"Should I use gels on him?"
You looked at me directly.
Tavakoly always used gels after a haircut.
Dust and dirt stuck to his hair
But he didn't take off the crown!
You say: "It's cool
I want my hair to stand up
Just like Superman!"
Thinking about Ajami, I ask:
"Is it easy to use?"
She takes a little bit of gels
And combs your hair back.

When we leave, I say:
"I plucked hair from my temples
To look like a grown-up."
You laugh and let the light
Fill your whole face.

October 26, 1995

---

[6] Tudeli: Children who cannot reach the
pedals from the seat, cross a leg to the opposite pedal beneath the crossbar.

43

EMPTY BED

Hearing a voice
I wake up, in the dark:
"Change the battery!
Change the battery!"

Is Azad coughing
Or asking for water
At his mom's house?

I turn off the voice
And return
To my empty bed.

January 20, 1997

THE PLACEMAT

Every morning,
I place my tea cup
On a checkered mat
Made by Azad,
Which appears today
As a chessboard.

Will Dad find a job?
Then he could buy you a house
And a Dalmatian
You would no longer envy our neighbor
Whose dog comes back from her walk
When you are going to school.
She wags her tail
Stands on her back legs
And leans aginst your chest
Looking directly into your eyes.

I move the sugar cube
From one square to another
And stare at your little pawns
Who are marching toward me
From the other side of the placemat.

August 3, 1997

POTTAGE

I cook the black-eyed peas
Until they become soft.
A handful of rice
A few drops of olive oil
One spoon of tomato sauce
A bit of salt and pepper
Green leaves of spinach
And white cloves of garlic
So charmingly asleep
In their bride's veils . . .
My pottage is ready to simmer.

I could be in a classroom now
Teaching poetry of Nima Yushij
In front of three dozen eyes;
Or in a safe house in Tehran
Which opens to opposite alleys
Discussing the new wave of revolt
In the circle of old comrades.

Yet, I am sitting here alone
thinking of my mother
Who every Saturday in winter
Made sour grape pottage.

The room is filled with familiar scents
And I know tonight,
When I walk Azad home
He will finish his bowl of pottage
And perhaps ask for an extra bowl.

Nobember 5, 1997

46

ALLOWANCE

When creeping out of his tight skin
He suffers pain
And the world becomes small for him.
I remember
that flimsy, fragile skin
left on a dewy rock
with two empty eye sockets
Looking inside
When you cry
And say: "I hate my life."
And I find
It is not only your sneakers and hat
and sport shorts that shrink
And I say: "OK!
I'll double your allowance."
And tonight
When you have left the house
and I am alone
I write these few lines
So that when you turn back
In search of your old skin
You'll find that today
August 10, 2000
It happened as described.

ABOUT THE AUTHOR

Majid Naficy was born in Iran in 1952. His first collection of poems in Persian called *In the Tiger's Skin*, was published in 1969. One year later his book of literary criticism, *Poetry as a Structure*, appeared. In 1971 he wrote a children's book, *The Secret of Words*, which won a national award in Iran.

In the 1970s, Majid was politically active against the Shah's regime. However, after the 1979 Revolution, the new regime began to suppress the opposition, and many people, including his first wife, Ezzat Tabaian and brother, Sa'id, were executed. He fled Iran in 1983 and spent a year and a half in Turkey and France. Majid then settled in Los Angeles where he lives with his son, Azad. He has since published five collections of poems, *After the Silence, Sorrow of the Border, Poems of Venice, Muddy Shoes,* and *Twelve Poems in Love: A Narrative* as well as two books of essays called *In Search of Joy: A Critique of Male-Dominated, Death-Oriented Culture in Iran,* and *Poetry & Politics and Twenty-Four Other Essays.* He is currently a co-editor of *Daftarhaya Kanoon,* a literary journal published by *The Iranian Writers' Association in Exile.*

Majid Naficy holds his doctorate in Near Eastern Languages and Cultures from the University of California at Los Angeles. His doctoral dissertation, *Modernism & Ideology in Persian Literature: A Return to Nature in the Poetry of Nima Yushij,* was published by University Press of America, Inc. in 1997.